Encounters with G...

The Second Epistle of Paul the Apostle to the CORINTHIANS

Encounters with God Study Guide Series

The Gospel of Matthew

The Gospel of Mark

The Gospel of Luke

The Gospel of John

The Book of Acts

The Book of Romans

The First Epistle of Paul the Apostle to the Corinthians

The Second Epistle of Paul the Apostle to the Corinthians

The Epistle of Paul the Apostle to the Galatians

The Epistle of Paul the Apostle to the Ephesians

The Epistle of Paul the Apostle to the Philippians

The Epistles of Paul the Apostle to the Colossians and Philemon

The First and Second Epistles of Paul the Apostle to the Thessalonians

The First and Second Epistles of Paul the Apostle to Timothy and Titus

The Epistle of Paul the Apostle to the Hebrews

The Epistle of James

The First and Second Epistles of Peter

The First, Second, and Third Epistles of John and Jude

The Revelation of Jesus Christ

Encounters with God

The Second Epistle of Paul the Apostle to the CORINTHIANS

Published in Nashville, Tennessee, by Thomas Nelson. Thomas Nelson is a registered trademark of Thomas Nelson, Inc.

Thomas Nelson, Inc. titles may be purchased in bulk for educational, business, fund-raising, or sales promotional use. For information, please e-mail SpecialMarkets@ThomasNelson.com.

All Scripture quotations are taken from THE NEW KING JAMES VERSION. © 1982 by Thomas Nelson, Inc. Used by permission. All rights reserved.

ISBN 978-1-4185-2645-0

Printed in the United States of America

HB 02.12.2024

CONTENTS

An Introduction to the Epistle of 2 Corinthians

The Book of 2 Corinthians is an "epistle"—a formal letter intended to give instruction. The letter was written by the apostle Paul to a vibrant, growing church in the Greek city of Corinth—a church that Paul had established several years before. The letter is closely linked in content to Paul's epistle known as 1 Corinthians, and it was likely written only a few months after that letter.

The letter that we know as 2 Corinthians was written while Paul was on his third missionary journey. During that third journey, Paul set out to revisit the churches that he had established on his second journey and he wrote to the Corinthians from "the road" as he traveled in Macedonia, perhaps writing from Philippi or Thessalonica. After writing the letter, Paul continued to travel to the borders of Illyricum and then, as promised in 2 Corinthians, he traveled to Corinth where he spent the winter months of 56–57 AD. This was actually Paul's THIRD visit to Corinth.

Paul is writing to people that he knows well, with a number of references to people and events that the people in Corinth knew well. Paul wrote the letter in advance of his personal visit in order that some remaining issues in the Corinthian church might be dealt with prior to his visit.

In truth, Paul's second visit to Corinth had not been pleasant. In 1 Corinthians Paul addressed several doctrinal and ethical problems in the church. He also sent his coworker Timothy to help the Corinthians (1 Corinthians 4:17) but apparently Timothy had not been able to correct the problems. Therefore, Paul had traveled from Ephesus directly to Corinth— a trip that he considered to be painful (2 Corinthians 2:1)—and he returned to Ephesus disheartened, sad, and humiliated. One man had taken the lead in defying Paul's spiritual authority over the congregation.

Once Paul returned to Ephesus, he wrote the Corinthians a strong disciplinary letter and sent it to the church with a coworker named Titus. Paul refers to this document in 2 Corinthians 2:3–4 and 7:8–9. (This letter has been lost in history).

Shortly after sending the letter with Titus, Paul embarked on his third missionary journey. He planned to rendezvous with Titus in Troas to learn more about the situation in Corinth (2 Corinthians 2:13). He waited in Troas until the last opportunity for travel across the Aegean before winter storms hit the sea. Then, recognizing that Titus would need to travel by land, he set sail and finally met up with him in Macedonia. Paul received good news about the general condition of the Corinthian church, but also bad news that a small faction continued to oppose his authority and teaching. This situation gave rise to the epistle that we know as 2 Corinthians.

In 2 Corinthians, Paul applauds the actions of the Corinthian church in dealing with those who opposed him and perhaps to vindicate himself further in their eyes, he explains his conduct and defends his own integrity. He reinforces the authenticity of both his apostleship and his message. The result is that 2 Corinthians is the most personal and intimate of all Paul's letters. It has more personal autobiographical references than any other epistle. The tone is loving and gentle for the first seven chapters, but then becomes quite severe as Paul seeks to deal with the remaining opposition in a decisive manner. The letter emphasizes obedience to Christ and respect and submission to Christ's messengers. A second strong theme is that of selfless giving, both in Christian service and in the sharing of personal possessions and resources. Paul certainly does not want his third visit with the Corinthians to be like his painful second visit—He longs for the believers there to be fully aware of all Satan's ploys and deceptions aimed at splintering the church. His desire is for reconciliation, which Paul contends is made possible as the Holy Spirit helps the Corinthian believers to remain focused on the love of Christ.

About the Author, the Apostle Paul. The author of this book, the apostle Paul, was in a unique position to write a theological letter to both Jewish and Gentile believers in Corinth. Paul, who received the Jewish name Saul at his birth, was born in the Roman city of Tarsus, located in Cilicia (Acts 22:3). A Hebrew by heritage, he grew up in Greek culture and obtained Roman citizenship. His family members, some of whom appear to have been wealthy and socially influential, were citizens of Rome. Saul received the finest education available and was a strong adherent to the Law of Moses. He became a Pharisee—the Pharisees were a leading and powerful sect in Judaism. He launched vicious attacks against the followers of Christ and was a witness to Stephen's stoning. It was while Saul was in zealous pursuit of the "followers of the Way" who had gone to Damascus, intending to persecute them even to the point of death, that he was blinded by a supernatural light and heard the voice of Jesus Christ (Acts 9:1–19). Confronted by Christ Himself, Saul's life was permanently redirected. He became as zealous a messenger for Christ as he once had been a persecutor of Christians. Changing his name to the Greek "Paul," he proclaimed Christ's "Good News" to the Gentiles with all-consuming passion, and in his lifetime, he launched at least four missionary journeys to spread the message of salvation and reconciliation with God made possible through Jesus Christ's crucifixion and resurrection. It was during his second missionary journey that he established the church in Corinth, spending a year and a half in the city. He was assisted in his ministry there by Silas and Timothy. On his third missionary journey, he also spent a period of weeks, perhaps several winter months, with the Corinthians.

AN OVERVIEW OF OUR STUDY OF THE EPISTLE OF 2 CORINTHIANS

This study guide presents seven lessons drawn from and based largely upon the Epistle of 2 Corinthians. The study guide elaborates upon, and is based upon, the commentary included in the *Blackaby Study Bible:*

Lesson #1: All Things Are "Yes" in Christ Jesus

Lesson #2: Forgiveness and Restoration

Lesson #3: Victorious in Persecution

Lesson #4: Assurance of the Resurrection

Lesson #5: Marks of Genuine Ministry

Lesson #6: Generosity in Giving

Lesson #7: God's Grace Is Sufficient

Personal or Group Use. These lessons are offered for personal study and reflection, or for small-group Bible study. The questions asked may be answered by an individual reader, or used as a foundation for group discussion. A segment titled "Notes to Leaders of Small Groups" is included at the back of this book to help those who might lead a group study of the material here.

Before you embark on this study, we encourage you to read in full the statement in the Blackaby Study Bible titled "How to Study the Bible." Our contention is always that the Bible is unique among all literature. It is God's definitive word for humanity. The Bible is:

- *inspired*—"God breathed"

- *authoritative*—absolutely the "final word" on any spiritual matter

- *the plumb line of truth*—the standard against which all human activity and reasoning must be evaluated

The Bible is fascinating in that it has remarkable diversity, but also remarkable unity. The books were penned by a diverse assortment of authors representing a variety of languages and cultures. The Bible as a whole has a number of literary forms. But, the Bible's message from cover to cover is clear, consistent, and unified.

More than mere words on a page, the Bible is an encounter with God Himself. No book is more critical to your life. The very essence of the Bible is the Lord Himself.

God speaks by the Holy Spirit through the Bible. He also communicates during your time of prayer, in your life circumstances, and through the church. Read your Bible in an attitude of prayer, and allow the Holy Spirit to make you aware of God's activity in your personal life. Write down what you learn, meditate on it, and adjust your thoughts, attitudes, and behavior accordingly. Look for ways every day in which the truth of God's Word can be applied to your circumstances and relationships. God is not random, but orderly and intentional in the way He speaks to you.

Be encouraged—the Bible is *not* too difficult for the average person to understand if that person asks the Holy Spirit for help. (Furthermore, not even the most brilliant person can fully understand the Bible apart from the Holy Spirit's help!) God desires for you to know Him and to know His Word. Every person who reads the Bible can learn from it. The person who will receive *maximum* benefit from reading and studying the Bible, however, is the person who:

- *is born again* (John 3:3, 5). Those who are born again and have received the gift of His Spirit have a distinct advantage in understanding the deeper truths of God's Word.

- *has a heart that desires to learn God's truth.* Your attitude influences greatly the outcome of Bible study. Resist the temptation to focus on what others have said about the Bible. Allow the Holy Spirit to guide you as you study God's Word for yourself.

- *a heart that seeks to obey God.* The Holy Spirit teaches most those who desire to apply what they learn.

Begin your Bible study with prayer, asking the Holy Spirit to guide your thoughts and to impress upon you what is on God's heart. Then make plans to adjust your life immediately to obey the Lord fully.

As you read and study the Bible, your purpose is not to *create* meaning, but to *discover* the meaning of the text with the Holy Spirit's guidance. Ask yourself, "What did the author have in mind? How was this applied by those who first heard these words?" Especially in your study of the Gospel accounts, pay attention to the words of Jesus that begin "truly, truly" or "He opened His mouth and taught them saying . . ." These are core principles and teachings that have powerful impact on *every* person's life.

At times you may find it helpful to consult other passages of the Bible (made available in the center columns in the Blackaby Study Bible), or the commentary that is in the margins of the Blackaby Study Bible.

Keep in mind always that Bible study is not primarily an exercise for acquiring information, but an opportunity for transformation. Bible study is your opportunity to encounter God and to be changed in His presence. When God speaks to your heart, nothing remains the same. Jesus said, "He who has ears to hear, let him hear" (Matt. 13:9). Choose to have ears that desire to hear!

The B-A-S-I-Cs of Each Study in This Guide. Each lesson in this study guide has five segments, using the word BASIC as an acronym. The word BASIC does not allude to elementary or "simple," but rather, to "foundational." These studies extend the concepts that are part of the Blackaby Study Bible commentary and are focused on key aspects of what it means to be a Christ-follower in today's world. The BASIC acronym stands for:

> *B* = *Bible Focus.* This segment presents the central passage for the lesson and a general explanation that covers the central theme or concern.

> *A* = *Application for Today.* This segment has a story or illustration related to modern-day times, with questions that link the Bible text to today's issues, problems, and concerns.

> *S* = *Supplementary Scriptures to Consider.* In this segment, other Bible verses related to the general theme of the lesson are explored.

> *I* = *Introspection and Implications.* In this segment, questions are asked that lead to deeper reflection about one's personal faith journey and life experiences.

> *C* = *Communicating the Good News.* In this segment, challenging questions are aimed at ways in which the truth of the lesson might be lived out and shared with others (either to win the lost or build up the church).

LESSON #1

ALL THINGS ARE "YES" IN CHRIST JESUS

Integrity: complete, undivided agreement between belief, word, and deed

B
Bible Focus

> And in this confidence I intended to come to you before,
> that you might have a second benefit—to pass by way of you
> to Macedonia, to come gain from Macedonia to you, and be
> helped by you on my way to Judea. Therefore, when I was
> planning this, did I do it lightly? Or the things I plan, did I
> plan according to the flesh, that with me there should be Yes,
> Yes, and No, No? But as God is faithful, our word to you was
> not Yes and No. For the Son of God, Jesus Christ, who was
> preached among you by us—by me, Silvanus, and Timothy—
> was not Yes and No, but in Him was Yes. For all the promises
> of God in Him are Yes, and in Him Amen, to the glory of
> God through us. Now He who establishes us with you in
> Christ and has anointed us is God, who also has sealed us
> and given us the Spirit in our hearts as a guarantee
> (2 Corinthians 1:15–22).

By the time Paul wrote the words above to the Corinthians, they were
criticizing him for stating that he was coming to visit them—twice, and then
changing his mind—twice. They accused him of saying "yes" and "no" in
the same breath. They had started voicing some concerns that perhaps they
couldn't trust *anything* that Paul had ever said to them.

Paul was quick to write, "I changed my plans because the Lord directed
me to change 3." He then added, "What I taught to you about Christ Jesus
has not, does not, and will not change. It was, is, and will always be absolute
truth without variation or change."

At the foundation are two deeper concerns that are held by many
Christians:

- What or who can be trusted?

- In a world of change, and a near constant volley between good and evil, is
  there anything that is permanent or perfect?

Paul answers both concerns. God does not change and His Word does not
change. God—Father, Son, and Holy Spirit—can be trusted at all times and
in all situations. The truth of our redemption in Christ Jesus is sealed within
us and is absolute. The Word of God is absolute truth and does not change
with the times. The perfection and infinite nature of God's goodness, wis-

dom, and love are fixed. Furthermore, God *always* seeks our eternal best and calls us to grow into the perfection of His plan and purposes.

What does this mean to us?

First, it means that we have a fixed point toward which we can navigate our way through all of life's choices and decisions. We do not need to go through life adrift. We can have direction, purpose, and meaning for our days.

Even if those we have loved and admired disappoint us or abandon us, God will not do so. Even if other people change, God does not. Ultimately, our faith must always be in the Lord, not in people.

Second, the absolute perfection and trustworthiness of God means that God is always calling us away from the "no" of sin and its ultimate downward spiral into degradation, despair, and death. He is always calling us toward the "yes" of life in Christ and the ultimate glory, joy, peace, and fulfillment to be found in Him.

God says to us at all times, "Yes, I will help you become like Jesus in character and I will help you make the choices and decisions that Jesus would make if He were walking in your shoes. Yes, I will be with you at all times and never leave you nor forsake you. Yes, I will work all things to your good as you trust in Me." Each and every time we make a choice to do things God's way, the Lord voices "Amen"—"so be it." He brings about a harvest from the seeds of faith that we plant and He causes good to come from our words and deeds, in spite of what outer circumstances seem to dictate. We can give our feeble attempts, and even our failed attempts, to God and trust that He will create good on our behalf and on the behalf of all His people.

We must guard closely against conversations or discussions that instill doubt about God's perfection or trustworthiness. We must guard closely against those debates that seek to undermine or dismiss the absolute nature of God's commandments.

People often believe that the most rational approach to any problem, need, decision or situation in our lives involves a careful analysis of the "pros and cons." We tend to admire those who can see—and to a degree, empathize with—both sides of an issue or relationship. We are frequently like the character Tevia in "Fiddler on the Roof" who debates within himself, "On the one hand..." but then quickly shifts to, "On the other hand...."

To some degree, the Corinthians had begun to *evaluate* their faith. They saw pros and cons to being a Christian. As a simple extension of this inner debate, they had also begun to evaluate Jesus, rather than simply believe in Him. They were beginning to wonder if Jesus had flaws to balance His superlative qualities. Paul knew how dangerous this was to them.

Paul made it very clear that Jesus was the *fulfillment* of all God's promises, and that the Word of God was absolute. Only a perfect Jesus can be the perfect sacrifice for sin. Only an absolute God can guarantee His promises. Only an authoritative and absolute expression of truth, the Bible, can be trusted. Do not allow other people to instill doubt in you. Choose to believe in the perfection and trustworthiness of your Savior and Lord.

A
Application for Today

A number of years ago, a Christian teacher working in a secular university had in one of her classes several students who were members of the university's debate team. She asked one of these students, "After debating both sides of this issue all year, what is *your* opinion on this issue?"

The student replied, "Which side of the proposition do you want me to argue?"

"Neither," the teacher replied. "I'd like to know what you personally have concluded after studying both sides."

The student stared at her blankly. He had no personal conclusion, although he was able to argue brilliantly both sides of the stated proposition.

At what point are we wise to focus on God's answers, rather than wallow in life's questions?

At what point are we wise to stop trying to "figure out" our faith, and simply *believe* in Christ Jesus?

At what point do we need to make a decision about Jesus? About being a Christian? About believing God's Word? About living for Christ?

At what point do we need to stop studying both sides of life, and take a stand for Christ?

S
Supplementary Scriptures to Consider

Jesus said:

"Let your 'Yes' be 'Yes,' and your 'No,' 'No' (Matthew 5:37).

- What is to be gained by making definitive, clear statements?

- Why do people tend to avoid absolutes or definitive language when we speak?

Paul also taught:

> Now may the God of peace Himself sanctify you completely;
> and may your whole spirit, soul, and body be preserved
> blameless at the coming of our Lord Jesus Christ.
> He who calls you is faithful, who also will do it
> (1 Thessalonians 5:23–24).

- What does it mean to you to be sanctified completely by the "God of peace"?

• What assurance do you feel in knowing that it is Jesus who is faithful in preserving us blameless?

• Is there anything you do *not* trust Jesus to do in you by the power of the Spirit?

The writer of Hebrews indicated that our part in averting a downward spiral of destruction is this:

> Let us lay aside every weight, and the sin which so easily ensnares us, and let us run with endurance the race that is set before us, looking unto Jesus, the author and finisher of our faith (Hebrews 12:1–2).

• How does the Lord *help* us lay aside every weight and sin?

- What is the "race" that has been set before us as Christians?

- In what practical ways might a person "look unto Jesus" to provide strength and energy to endure the race before us?

I
Introspection and Implications

1. Have you ever experienced difficulty in trusting God in a particular situation or in a specific relationship? Why do you believe that was so? What did you do, or what might you do?

2. Whom do you trust to be a constant in your life—something of a "fixed North Star"?

3. In what ways do you find it difficult to maintain consistency in your faith walk? In spiritual disciplines such as prayer and reading the Bible?

4. Does anything about the concept "absolute truth" trouble you? If so, do you know why you feel troubled?

5. Where do you turn when you need a definitive "yes" or "no" answer to a question or choice?

6. Is there benefit to asking God "yes" or "no" questions in seeking God's guidance?

C
Communicating the Good News

What are the things that we need to "know without doubt" as we present the Gospel message to someone who is without Christ Jesus?

Are there particular words that we tend to use in evangelistic messages that may be ambiguous or without meaning to an unbeliever? Why are we wise to avoid these words?

To what degree to you believe it is vital to be consistent and trustworthy as we present Christ Jesus to an unsaved world?

LESSON #2

FORGIVENESS AND RESTORATION

Reconciliation: the end of conflict and the renewal of a friendly relationship between disputing parties Restore: to bring something back to an earlier or better condition, or to reestablish or put back something that once was but is no longer there

B
Bible Focus

*This punishment which was inflicted by the majority is suffi-
cient for such a man, so that, on the contrary, you ought
rather to forgive and comfort him, lest perhaps such a one be
swallowed up with too much sorrow. Therefore I urge you to
reaffirm your love to him. For to this end I also wrote, that I
might put you to the test, whether you are obedient in all
things. Now whom you forgive anything, I also forgive. For if
indeed I have forgiven anything, I have forgiven that one for
your sakes in the presence of Christ, lest Satan should take
advantage of us; for we are not ignorant of his devices
(2 Corinthians 2:6–11).*

The apostle Paul had been criticized openly, publicly, and apparently
harshly by someone within the Corinthian church. We do not know all of the
details, but we can conclude several important things from this very short
passage:

First, even the most powerful, effective, and godly preachers of the Gospel
experience unwarranted criticism. That is not to say that preachers are
without fault. Certainly every person has faults and every person fails from
time to time. No man or woman, apart from Jesus Christ, is or ever will be
perfect as long as that person lives on this earth. The point made here is that
every person experiences unfair and unnecessary criticism from time to time.
The criticism may be regarding the person's performance or skills, personal-
ity or character, appearance or mannerisms, or leadership decisions. We may
be called to judge the fruit of a person's behavior and the validity of a
person's message, but we are never to judge another person as being worthy
or unworthy of God's love and redemption. Such judgment belongs solely to
God (See Luke 6:36).

Second, unfair and unnecessary criticism not only brings harm to the
person being criticized, but it brings harm to the entire church. Criticism
breeds doubt, discord, and disagreement—all of which produce divisions and
factions that tear away at the unity that God desires to be the atmosphere of
the church. When divisiveness is the norm, a church no longer experiences
the full flow of the Holy Spirit, and ultimately, divisiveness becomes coun-
terproductive to the edification of the saints and evangelism of the lost. A
church that is filled with expressions of encouragement, love, and support is
strong—lost souls can't wait to be part of such a body! On the other hand, a
church that is filled with rancor and criticism is a church that is likely losing
its most godly members and attracting no new ones.

Third, when unfair or unnecessary criticism is brought under the strong spotlight of truth, a backlash very often occurs. This was the case in Corinth. Paul had been unjustly criticized and the majority in the church had "turned" against the critic, perhaps even to the point of shunning him completely or ostracizing him from various church functions. Paul's response: forgive the offending critic and reaffirm your godly love for him. (Remember that it is to this very church that Paul wrote 1 Corinthians 13, an amazing statement on godly love).

Fourth, forgiveness is the antidote for every spiritual illness in the church. Forgiveness and love send the devil fleeing. Forgiveness and love are the foundation for true reconciliation and restoration.

Paul notes that one of the foremost devices of Satan is to instill a spirit of criticism in the church, and then to allow that spirit of criticism to result in rejection and alienation. We must not let it happen! We must be at all times agents of forgiveness and love, inviting God to knit our hearts and lives together so that we might be effective witnesses of the Gospel.

A
Application for Today

George was sure that he was right and the pastor was wrong. He said so openly during a conversation with Bill, Joe, Terrance, and Carlos. They went home and passed on George's criticism to their wives, Leta, Jen, Lakeesha, and Maria. The wives got together and talked about what their husbands had said. Leta and Jen sided with the pastor, Lakeesha and Maria sided with George. Leta and Bill disagreed; so did Carlos and Maria. Joe and Terrance were in agreement with their wives.

Maria reiterated the criticism to the choir, Lakeesha to the meeting of Sunday school teachers, Bill to the ushers, and Terrance to the church softball team.

The second baseman on the softball team and third-grader's Sunday school teacher told the pastor what was going on. He called George and confronted him about his allegations. George denied that he had said anything to anybody, and then further criticized the "heavy handed" methods of the pastor, and labeled him an "incompetent leader" and eventually a "jerk." Some in the church agreed with these assessments, others rose to the defense of the pastor, saying that no matter WHAT the pastor may have done in the past, he didn't deserve those labels. Still others got sick and tired of the swirling criticism and decided that they'd try attending the church down the street. Some rose to the defense of the pastor and began to openly criticize George and anybody who sided with him. The pastor didn't know where to

turn or what to do. His denominational supervisor had pitifully few sugges-
tions about what to do.

Eventually, facing declining church attendance and lower offering "in-
come," the church board called a church-wide meeting. George refused to
attend and submitted a letter of resignation from the church. The pastor
made a plea for unity, forgiveness, and reconciliation. Some said, "Amen."
Several voiced hope that George would change his mind and suggested
measures to reach out to him. Others said, "Let him go and good riddance."

What a mess!

And what to do NOW?

S
Supplementary Scriptures to Consider

Paul wrote this about the convicting power of the Holy Spirit to turn us
toward godly living:

> Now I rejoice, not that you were made sorry, but that your
> sorrow led to repentance. For you were made sorry in a godly
> manner, that you might suffer loss from us in nothing. For
> godly sorrow produces repentance leading to salvation, not to
> be regretted (2 Corinthians 7:9–10).

• What is a repentant heart? Describe the practical manifestations of
  repentance.

• What does it mean to be "sorry in a godly manner"?

Jesus taught:

> Be merciful, just as your Father also is merciful. Judge not,
> and you shall not be judged. Condemn not, and you shall
> not be condemned. Forgive, and you will be forgiven"
> (Luke 6:36–37).

- As Christians, we are called elsewhere in the Scriptures to judge behavior as being "right or wrong." Jesus admonished His followers, however, to avoid judging people as "good" or "bad." In what ways is it difficult to differentiate between what a person does and what a person "is"?

- To condemn is to determine that a person cannot be redeemed. Are there people on the earth today that you believe are beyond redemption? Why so?

- What is your working definition for *forgiveness*?

• What is your working definition for being *merciful*?

• How do forgiveness and mercy differ?

• Can you have forgiveness but not be reconciled?

Paul taught this about the transforming power of the Holy Spirit:

> If anyone is in Christ, he is a new creation; old things have passed away; behold, all things have become new. Now all things are of God, who has reconciled us to Himself through Jesus Christ, and has given us the ministry or reconciliation, that is, that God was in Christ reconciling the world to Himself, not imputing their trespasses to them, and has committed to us the word of reconciliation.

Now then, we are ambassadors for Christ, as though God
were pleading through us: we implore you on Christ's behalf,
be reconciled to God. For He made Him who knew no sin to
be sin for us, that we might become the righteousness of God
in Him (2 Corinthians 5:17–21).

• What is truly made "new" when we come to Christ? Is there anything that
  remains "old" in us? If so, what?

• What does it mean to "become the righteousness of God" through Jesus
  Christ?

I
Introspection and Implications

1. How have you personally experienced the "convicting" power of the
   Holy Spirit in your life?

2. What do you believe keeps a person from being instantly repentant when he or she knows that she has broken God's commandments or hurt another human being?

3. Have you experienced unfair criticism? How did you handle that situation?

4. Have you ever been caught up in the swirling rumors and opinions of a church divided about a particular issue? What was the result?

5. Why do we human beings seem to defend our "rights" and our "opinions" to the point of destroying a relationship that we say we value?

6. What role does criticism have in the church, if any?

C
Communicating the Good News

How do you respond to this statement: "God forgives unconditionally out of the wellspring of His unconditional love"? In what ways does this statement challenge us in our forgiveness and love of fellow believers? Of the lost?

How best might we as a church present the message of God's love and forgiveness to a lost world?

How best might we *model* for the world a message of God's love and forgiveness?

LESSON #3

VICTORIOUS IN PERSECUTION

Persecution: deliberate cruel or unfair treatment often involving genuine suffering

B
Bible Focus

> But we have this treasure in earthen vessels, that the
> excellence of the power may be of God and not of us. We are
> hard-pressed on every side, yet not crushed; we are perplexed,
> but not in despair; persecuted, but not forsaken; struck down,
> but not destroyed—always carrying about in the body the
> dying of the Lord Jesus, that the life of Jesus also may be
> manifested in our body. For we who live are always delivered
> to death for Jesus' sake, that the life of Jesus also may be
> manifested in our mortal flesh. So then death is working in us,
> but life in you. And since we have the same spirit of faith,
> according to what is written, "I believed and therefore I
> spoke," we also believe and therefore speak, knowing that He
> who raised up the Lord Jesus will also raise us up with Jesus,
> and will present us with you. For all things are for your sakes,
> that grace, having spread through the many, may cause
> thanksgiving to abound to the glory of God.
>
> Therefore we do not lose heart. Even though our outward
> man is perishing, yet the inward man is being renewed day by
> day. For our light affliction, which is but for a moment, is
> working for us a far more exceeding and eternal weight of
> glory, while we do not look at the things which are seen, but at
> the things which are not seen. For the things which are seen
> are temporary, but the things which are not see are eternal
> (2 Corinthians 4:7–18).

Few people in history have endured as much persecution and both physical and emotional anguish as the apostle Paul. Even so, when Paul compared his earthly suffering with eternal glory, his sufferings paled into insignificance. Paul did not deny his troubles, and he never suggested that the Corinthians or any other body of believers should deny that they were suffering. Rather, he called those who were being persecuted to regard their suffering in a new light, and to see their sufferings as having purpose and benefit.

Paul made three powerful statements to the Corinthians:

First, Paul reminded the believers in Corinth that as human beings, we all are "earthen vessels." We are fashioned from the dust of the earth—indeed, our bodies have the same chemicals as the earth's soil. We nevertheless are entrusted to be vessels that bear the presence of Christ Jesus into the world. Paul lived in a culture in which small pottery jars were used to hold oil and lamp wicks. These little vessels could be purchased for pennies, but the light that the lamps cast once they were lit changed everything in the immediate environment. So, too, we are to be filled with the light of Christ and change the world around us.

Second, Paul encouraged the believers in Corinth that persecutions and suffering affects only the outer man. A person can live victoriously on the "inside" in spite of dire external circumstances.

We are the ones who determine how we will respond emotionally, mentally, and spiritually to life's trials and tribulations. We may be hard-pressed by life's problems, but we do not need to be crushed in our spirit. We may face perplexing challenges, but we do not need to be overwhelmed by them. We may be put down or rejected by people, but we are never forsaken by God. We may be hit hard by evil, but the enemy of our souls cannot destroy our eternal relationship with almighty God. What good news this is! We need to remind ourselves daily that, although we face hardships in this life, the way we handle them sends a message that has eternal consequences. When we handle life's difficulties with faith, our witness can be potent.

Third, Paul extended hope to the believers in Corinth that all troubles and trials are temporary. This life is *not* all there is. We may become less and less physically, especially as we age, but we are empowered by the Holy Spirit to become more and more spiritually.

Are you facing a difficult situation today?

No matter what the nature of that difficulty, hear Paul saying to you, "Do not lose heart!"

The way you handle this time of trouble in your life may be the very example that God uses to win a lost soul or to encourage another person. The trouble is temporary. The impact of the way you *handle* the trouble may be eternal.

A
Application for Today

"Why, God?"

It is a question that most people ask, even those mighty in faith, when life deals them a strong blow. The death of a young child, the sin of a spouse, the rebellion of a teenager, failure in a career or business venture, the diagnosis of a deadly disease . . . the tragedies of our lives come in many sizes and shapes. The feelings that we have in the wake of tragedy are generally ones of deep sorrow and despair. We often reel in pain and desperately cry out, "Why?" Very often, we receive no answer to our question.

Have you ever asked God, "Why?"

Have you ever felt even greater pain when you failed to receive an answer from God that satisfied your aching heart?

What are the questions that we should ask?

Consider these:

- "What now?"

- "What am I to learn from this?"

How should I live during this time to give testimony of my faith to others?"

- "How might I help others around me, especially those who may be hurting as much as I am?"

These four questions are ones that turn us upward and outward, rather than downward and inward.

What response should we make to times of suffering? Time and again the psalmist poured out his anguish to the Lord, and then concluded his song, "Blessed be the name of the Lord."

God hears our cries. He empathizes with our pain. He has a plan and purpose, which we may never understand this side of eternity. And in the end, our *healing* from a difficult time comes when we praise His name.

Have you ever experienced the power of praise to heal your hurting heart?

S
Supplementary Scriptures to Consider

The Psalmist knew persecution, and he also knew what it meant to trust God for enduring strength and deliverance from persecution:

> How long, O Lord? Will You forget me forever?
> How long will You hide Your face from me?
> How long shall I take counsel in my soul,
> Having sorrow in my heart daily?
> How long will my enemy be exalted over me?
> Consider and hear me, O Lord my God;
> Enlighten my eyes,
> Lest I sleep the sleep of death;
> Lest my enemy say,
> "I have prevailed against him".
> Lest those who trouble me rejoice when I am moved.

> But I have trusted in Your mercy,
> My heart shall rejoice in Your salvation.
> I will sing to the LORD,
> Because He has dealt bountifully with me (Psalm 13).

• Have you ever felt the way the psalmist seemed to feel? What caused you to feel this way? How did you deal with your feelings?

• Have you ever struggled with trusting God during a time of persecution or trial?

What did you do?

The Psalmist wrote:

> The LORD tests the righteous,
> But the wicked and the one who loves violence His soul
> hates.

> Upon the wicked He will rain coals;
> Fire and brimstone and a burning wind
> Shall be the portion of their cup.
> For the LORD is righteous,
> He loves righteousness;
> His countenance beholds the upright (Psalm 11:5–7).

- What are God's purposes in "testing" the righteous? Is it so that the person being tested might be informed of his own weaknesses and need for God? Is it to bring about change in the person's life?

- What do you say to the person who claims that God is incapable of hate or harm?

- What is your practical definition for righteousness?

• In what ways is our righteousness tested in times of persecution or suffering?

The Psalmist had only one place to go for refuge in the midst of his persecution:

> When my spirit was overwhelmed within me,
> Then You knew my path.
> In the way in which I walk
> They have secretly set a snare for me.
> Look on my right hand and see,
> For there is no one who acknowledges me;
> Refuge has failed me;
> No one cares for my soul.
> I cried out to You, O LORD:
> I said, "You are my refuge;
> My portion in the land of the living.
> Attend to my cry.
> For I am brought very low;
> Deliver me from my persecutors,
> For they are stronger than I.
> Bring my soul out of prison,
> That I may praise Your name;
> The righteous shall surround me,
> For You shall deal bountifully with me" (Psalm 142:3–7).

• To what or to whom do you turn when you are feeling "overwhelmed" by life?

- How do you pray when you are feeling persecuted or are suffering?

- What does the phrase "bring my soul out of prison" mean to you?

I
Introspection and Implications

1. Every person experiences difficulties and times of suffering or sorrow. How have you dealt with those times in your life?

2. What lessons have you learned through "difficult times" that you did not seem to learn through "easy times"?

3. Has anyone ever "secretly set a snare" against you? How did you respond?

4. In what ways have your own difficult experiences helped you to be more empathetic and of greater help to others who may be experiencing a similar difficult time?

5. In what ways have times of testing or trial strengthened your faith? Why do you believe some people don't seem to grow stronger in their faith during difficult times?

6. Consider this statement: "God's *presence* is God's answer to us in times of personal tragedy and pain—His presence is far more potent than any answer that He might convey to our minds."

C
Communicating the Good News

How is "God's help" a critical factor in evangelism, especially to those who are suffering, experiencing persecution, or are going through a very difficult time? To what degree are those who are suffering or experiencing great need more receptive to the Gospel than those who are "on top of the world"?

Where might you go to find people who are suffering within a radius of ten miles of your home or church?

LESSON #4

ASSURANCE OF THE RESURRECTION

Tent: temporary covering or dwelling

B
Bible Focus

> For we know that if our earthly house, this tent, is de-
> stroyed, we have a building from God, a house not made with
> hands, eternal in the heavens. For in this we groan, earnestly
> desiring to be clothed with our habitation which is from
> heaven, if indeed, having been clothed, we shall not be found
> naked. For we who are in this tent groan, being burdened, not
> because we want to be unclothed, but further clothed, that
> mortality may be swallowed up by life. Now He who has
> prepared us for this very thing is God, who also has given us
> the Spirit as a guarantee.
>
> So we are always confident, knowing that while we are at
> home in the body we are absent from the Lord. For we walk by
> faith, not by sight. We are confident, yes, well pleased rather
> to be absent from the body and to be present with the Lord
>
> (2 Corinthians 5:1–8).

Paul was not afraid to die. For him, death meant freedom from the con-
straints of his physical body and the persecution of those who did not value
his ministry or rejected his message. For him, death meant entering into the
near presence of the Lord—Paul saw death as a promotion, reward, and
blessing. He wrote to the Corinthians that he preferred the option of dying to
living.

Note especially that Paul indicated that God is preparing us for a "further
clothing" of His presence. The presence of the Holy Spirit that we may
experience in this life is only a foretaste of an even greater exhilaration that
we will enjoy in the presence of God the Father.

Have you ever stopped to consider that everything God allows to happen
to you in your present life is part of His greater plan to *prepare* you for your
eternal future? God is at work continually to prepare you to be the person
with whom He desires to live forever!

What lessons does He seem to be teaching you—directly from His word
or through the experiences that you are currently facing?

What changes in your character is He fashioning—what changes can you
see as you look back on recent years, or as you look back over your entire
walk with the Lord?

What purpose do you see now for certain events in your past—perhaps
events that were painful and seemed to have NO purpose as you were
experiencing them?

Do you have a joy in your heart about what God has prepared for you in eternity?

All of life's lessons are temporary.

They are preparing us for a life that is eternal.

A
Application for Today

"What are your classes this fall?" a father asked as he put down his newspaper and looked up from his easy chair. His daughter was walking through the room, soon to leave for her sophomore year in college, her major still undeclared.

His daughter stopped and sat on the edge of his chair. She listed her classes, including one called "The Rise and Fall of Elegance."

"What does THAT cover?" the father asked.

"I don't know," his daughter replied as she leaned over to kiss her father's forehead. "But it's three credits of elective and I heard someone say it is an easy A and I'm sure I'll learn *something*."

As she left the room, she heard her father sigh, "For this I spend $250 a credit hour. . . ."

The broader classroom of life offers many courses, some of which are electives, some of which are expensive (not only financially), and some of which are fun. The question that we are wise to ask, however, is always this: "In what ways will learning this or doing this count for eternity?"

Seeing life through the lens of eternity causes us to confront our *purpose* for living. It makes us more intentional, more focused on what has lasting meaning.

Which of the things that you do regularly have the greatest meaning for you? Which relationships are most rewarding or fulfilling? How do these activities or relationships give you purpose in your life?

What do you believe God wants you still to learn before you die?

S
Supplementary Scriptures to Consider

Paul wrote with great confidence about our personal resurrection after death:

> If the Spirit of Him who raised Jesus from the dead dwells in you, He who raised Christ from the dead will also give life to our mortal bodies through His Spirit who dwells in you (Romans 8:11).

- Throughout the Scriptures the Lord is called the "giver of life." Jesus referred to Himself as the "the way, the truth, and the life." What does it mean to you that the eternal giver of life resides "in you" after your received Jesus as your Savior?

- What do you believe to be the "quantity" of life that Jesus imparts to you?

- What do you believe to be the "quality" of life that Jesus imparts? How does that quality of life change in eternity, or does it?

Paul wrote to Timothy, his colleague in ministry, these reassuring words:

> This is a faithful saying:
> For if we died with Him,
> We shall also live with Him.
> If we endure,
> We shall also reign with Him (2 Timothy 2:11–12).

• What does it mean to you to "reign" with Christ Jesus?

• How is it that we have already "died" with Christ?

John described a vision he experienced:

> Now when He had taken the scroll, the four living creatures and the twenty-four elders fell down before the Lamb, each having a harp, and golden bowls full of incense, which are the prayers of the saints. And they sang a new song, saying:
>
>> "You are worthy to take the scroll,
>> And to open its seals;
>> For You were slain,
>> And have redeemed us to God by Your blood
>> Out of every tribe and tongue and people and nation,
>> And have made us kings and priests to our God;
>> And we shall reign on the earth" (Revelation 5:8–10).

• What does it mean to you to be a "king and priest" to God?

- What does it mean to you that "we shall reign on the earth"?

- Is this praise song for Jesus only for eternity, or is it for us as believers today?

- Our praise of Christ Jesus is the one activity that we do now on earth that we will continue to do in heaven. How vital is praising the Lord to you?

I
Introspection and Implications

1. Do you fear death? Why or why not?

2. Are you looking forward to heaven? Why or why not?

3. Paul wrote that God is the One who has prepared us for mortality to be swallowed up by life and that He "has given us the Spirit as a guarantee." What does this mean to you personally?

C
Communicating the Good News

What role does the assurance of a heavenly home and eternal life play in our evangelistic efforts?

How do you counter the argument made by some that *all* who die—regardless of their rejection or acceptance of Jesus—go to heaven, if not directly, at least eventually?

Many people do not take seriously their eternal destiny until they are near death or until they encounter the death of a loved one. How might we aim our evangelistic efforts toward those who are dying, or struggling with a fear of dying?

Lesson #5
Marks of Genuine Ministry

Ministry: to help a person in need Christian Ministry: to help a needy person in the Name of Christ Jesus

B
Bible Focus

> *We give no offense in anything, that our ministry may not be blamed. But in all things we commend ourselves as ministers of God: in much patience, in tribulations, in needs, in distresses, in stripes, in imprisonments, in tumults, in labors, in sleeplessness, in fastings; by purity, by knowledge, by longsuffering, by kindness, by the Holy Spirit, by sincere love, by the word of truth, by the power of God, by the armor of righteousness on the right hand and on the left, by honor and dishonor, by evil report and good report, as deceivers, and yet true; as unknown, and yet well known, as dying, and behold we live; as chastened, and yet not killed, as sorrowful, yet always rejoicing; as poor, yet making many rich; as having nothing, and yet possessing all things (2 Corinthians 6:3–1).*

Do you consider yourself to be a minister?

You are if you are a believer in Christ Jesus!

Certainly not every believer is a clergy person, or a person in church leadership. But every Christian is called to help others in need and that is what "ministry" is—an act of help to somebody in need. Needs vary widely—from emotional and mental, to physical and financial, to relational and spiritual. Acts of ministry that address various needs also vary widely, from a monetary donation to full-time care-giving, from speaking and counseling to simply being "present" in a moment of crisis, from emergency medical care to making a phone call.

Paul admonished the Corinthians that they should have a goal of giving no reason for offense to unbelievers, or to their fellow Christians. Rather, he set out for them the profile of a mature minister—a profile that he had personally lived out and which he admonished them to follow. Note the marks of this profile:

- patient with others and with the unfolding plan of God

- willing to endure tribulations, and times of intense needs or stress

- faithful even if publicly punished or imprisoned

- calm in times of intense conflict

- willing to work hard and put in long hours

- engaging frequently in fasting and prayer

- a life of purity

- studying God's Word diligently

- bearing with "difficult others" and showing kindness to them

- led by the Holy Spirit

- expressing sincere love

- giving to others the truth of God, in the power of God

- a righteous life

- steady even if ridiculed or overlooked

- steady even if given great honor or recognition

- countering all lies with an exemplary life

- knowing that God sees all and is the final judge of all

- having assurance of "riches in glory" and authority in Christ Jesus

- having confidence of God's love and eternal life regardless of persecutions

Does this profile seem impossible to duplicate? Does this profile indicate that a person needs to be perfect before he or she might minister to others? Not at all!

Look more closely at these hallmarks of a mature minister. They are hallmarks of behavior that every Christian *can* develop. They are marks against which we can evaluate ourselves, and perhaps most potently, they are points for prayer!

If you see that you fall short in one of these areas, ask the Holy Spirit to help you "grow up" in your abilities to minister to others and especially to help you become stronger in that area of perceived weakness. Every Christian minister, no matter how old or how mature, can *increase* in each of these areas as they seek to help others in need.

Identify areas in which you believe the Holy Spirit is challenging you to become more mature.

Identify specific disciplines that you may need to incorporate into your life—for example, more prayer, more reading of God's Word, eliminating some activities from your life, changing some habits.

Lay this template of mature ministry next to the formal or informal job description associated with your "ministry." Identify ways in which you might minister to others with greater spiritual authority and maturity.

We are saved to serve.

We are blessed to be a blessing.

We receive ministry in order to give ministry.

Seek to become the best possible minister of God's love to those who are desperate for help.

A
Application for Today

"I quit."

That's all Marilee put in her note to the person in charge of the "outreach" ministries at her church. Marilee had been the coordinator of several practical areas of ministry, including meals to grieving families, transportation for the elderly to doctor appointments, and giving bouquets made from altar arrangements to those who were homebound.

Marilee's supervisor, Anna, was quick to go to Marilee's home to talk to her about her resignation. "Why?" Anna asked.

Marilee sighed deeply. "I'm 70. I'm too old for this. Somebody else needs to step up and take over."

Anna, "Do you need more help? Surely you can stay in this position for a little longer to train other people to take over your responsibilities."

Marilee stared out the window. "It's a thankless job. I can't imagine who would want to take over these jobs."

Anna suddenly had several flashes of insight into the real problems underlying Marilee's resignation. Marilee had not received enough thanks and recognition for her work, and she therefore was feeling overwhelmed and underappreciated. Even more, Marilee had been dealing with the families of many of her friends, who now were too old and sick to drive, were homebound, and were dying. Marilee was a mature believer, but in all likelihood, for the last several years she had been "giving out" far more than she had been "taking in" what she needed to maintain spiritual strength.

If you were Anna, how would you counsel Marilee?

How do you keep from burning out in your ministry?

What are the difficulties that arise when a person who is "burned out" on a particular ministry remains in the position of ministry, but without joy and with an increased feeling of bitterness and resentment?

S
Supplementary Scriptures to Consider

The apostle Paul was actually criticized by some for not "charging" for his ministerial services!

> For I consider that I am not at all inferior to the most eminent apostles. Even though I am untrained in speech, yet I am not in knowledge. But we have been thoroughly manifested among you in all things.
>
> Did I commit sin in humbling myself that you might be exalted, because I preached the gospel of God to you free of charge? I robbed other churches, taking wages from them to minister to you. And when I was present with you, and in need, I was a burden to no one, for what I lacked the brethren who came from Macedonia supplied. And in everything I kept myself from being burdensome to you, and so I will keep myself. As the truth of Christ is in me, no one shall stop me from this boasting in the regions of Achaia. Why? Because I do not love you? God knows!
>
> But what I do, I will also continue to do, that I may cut off the opportunity from those who desire an opportunity to be regarded just as we are in the things of which they boast. For such are false apostles, deceitful workers, transforming themselves into apostles of Christ. And no wonder! For Satan himself transforms himself into an angel of light. Therefore it is no great thing if his ministers also transform themselves into ministers of righteousness, whose end will be according to their works (2 Corinthians 11:5–15).

• What are the advantages of ministering to others totally "free of charge"?

- Those who were criticizing Paul were charging high prices for their ministry. They claimed that their ministry was of great "value" and that those who minister without charge actually have little regard for their own talents or for the recipients of their ministry. How would you address this argument if it was leveled against your ministry?

- In what ways might a person "transform himself" into a minister of righteousness when he actually bears no righteousness? What are the trappings of "ministry" that people tend to associate with piety? Why are these trappings unreliable indicators?

Paul considered his colleague Timothy to be a mature minister. He wrote to the church at Philippi about Timothy:

> I trust in the Lord Jesus to send Timothy to you shortly, that I also may be encouraged when I know your state. For I have no one like-minded, who will sincerely care for your state. For all seek their own, not the things which are of Christ Jesus. But you know his proven character, that as a son with his father he served with me in the gospel (Philippians 2:19–22).

- How can we "prove" the character of another person?

- Why is it especially important to seek church leaders of proven character?

- What are the "things which are of Christ Jesus"? Why is it important that the leader of a church be focused on the "things which are of Christ Jesus"?

I
Introspection and Implications

1. Take another look at the hallmarks of a mature minister. In what areas are you strong? In what areas do you desire to mature even more? How will you seek to develop stronger ministry ability?

2. Does a person ever retire from ministry as a Christian?

3. Is there a difference in the "ministry" profile of a professional clergy person and a lay person?

4. How might a church guard itself against a false minister? What should be done if a church recognizes that it is being led by someone who is not a genuine servant of the Lord Jesus Christ?

5. Have your abilities to minister to others changed through the years? In what ways? Has your role in ministry within your church changed over time? How so?

C
Communicating the Good News

Many people tend to leave "ministry" to paid clergy, and evangelism to "professional evangelists." What would Paul have said to those who hold such opinions?

As we win the lost to Christ Jesus and make disciples of all nations, in what ways should we be challenging new converts to "grow up" into mature ministers?

LESSON #6

GENEROSITY IN GIVING

Generous: pleasingly, freely, and willingly ready to give money, help, or time in sufficient quantities for genuine help

B
Bible Focus

But this I say: He who sows sparingly will also reap sparingly, and he who sows bountifully will also reap bountifully. So let each one give as he purposes in his heart, not grudgingly or of necessity; for God loves a cheerful giver. And God is able to make all grace abound toward you, that you, always having all sufficiency in all things, may have an abundance for every good work. As it is written:

"He has dispersed abroad,
He has given to the poor
His righteousness endures forever" (Psalm 112:9).

Now may He who supplies seed to the sower, and bread for food, supply and multiply the seed you have sown and increase the fruits of your righteousness, while you are enriched in everything for all liberality, which causes thanksgiving through us to God. For the administration of this service not only supplies the needs of the saints, but also is abounding through many thanksgiving to God, while, through the proof of this ministry, they glorify God for the obedience of your confession to the gospel of Christ, and for your liberal sharing with them and all men, and by their prayer for you, who long for you because of the exceeding grace of God in you (2 Corinthians 9:6–14).

The cycle of seedtime and harvest is one of the great "laws" in the natural world. This law applies not only to farming, but to all acts of giving or planting. One corollary to the law of seedtime and harvest is the "law of generosity." The more one gives, the greater one's harvest.

A second corollary is this: God "supplies seed to the sower and bread for food." God has given to every person *something* which that person might plant or give. No person is totally bereft of giving ability, even if only a smile, a word of encouragement, or a note of appreciation. God also is the one who produces ALL harvests. No person can make a seed grow or produce. No person can make an investment increase or a gift multiply. Only God turns what we give into a need-meeting harvest, and He is faithful at all times to provide for His people. He is worthy of our praise in this!

The apostle Paul also calls attention to these aspects of giving:

• Our attitude toward giving is important.

• God desires that we have more than "sufficiency"—He desires that we have an abundance so that we can give generously to others.

Very specifically, Paul notes that God loves a "cheerful" giver. A little earlier in his letter to the Corinthians, Paul cited the example of the believers in Macedonia. Even though they had experienced great affliction and were poor, they had taken the initiative to give generously toward those who were in need in Jerusalem (See Galatians 2:10, Romans 15:25–28). Paul wrote of them, "I bear witness that according to their ability, yes, and beyond their ability, they were freely willing, imploring us with much urgency that we would receive the gift and the fellowship of the ministering to the saints. And not only as we had hoped, but they first gave themselves to the Lord, and then to us by the will of God" (2 Corinthians 8:3–5).

Truly there is joy in helping another person! When we give out of obligation we feel burdened and obligated. When we give to help someone we feel joy. Always keep in mind the end goal of your giving—get a clear picture of the person you are helping—and you *will* have greater joy in giving. The more real the person being helped and the more intense their need, the more generous your giving is likely to become.

The purpose of giving is never to drain completely those who are wealthy (whether financially, materially, emotionally, or spiritually "rich"). The purpose of giving generously is that we might experience a generous "inflow" into our lives to replenish, replace, and restore us. Freely flowing water doesn't stagnate. In like manner, a continual flow of receiving and giving creates an ongoing "freshness" to our lives—a purpose, a sense of fulfillment, and a sense of enthusiasm. The more we give, the wider the riverbanks of our giving become. We benefit, even as others benefit. There is a mutual sufficiency to the point of mutual overflow, so that what we need we receive *fully*, and what we give *fully* meets the needs of others. We go from increase to increase, from greater to even greater ability to give.

Only God can make this happen. Only God can turn a seed into an abundant harvest. Only God can impart a genuine sense of joy and fulfillment to our lives. He asks that we sow what we have. He gives the increase.

In what ways has God caused your life to increase as you have given?

What challenges do you personally face in giving, or in giving generously?

How do you "feel" about giving?"

In what ways are you feeling challenged to give more?

A
Application for Today

Walter had a problem and he went to his pastor with it. "People are always asking for money," Walter said. Then he paused for a moment and added with a glare, "Even you preachers!"

The pastor sat back in his chair for a moment. Walter was a wealthy man. He had inherited a sizeable amount of money and a successful business, and he had turned his inheritance into a small fortune. Walter also was a faithful giver to the church. The pastor had no idea that he resented giving, or that he felt it was a burden. While he felt momentarily attacked, the pastor refused to become defensive. He had no guilt in asking others to give generously to the work of the Lord or to the needs in the church. He began to pray silently for the right words to say to Walter. Finally, he said this:

"It's a problem, alright."

"Glad you agree," Walter said.

"What are you asking for?" the pastor said.

"I'm not asking for ANYTHING from ANYONE," Walter said strongly.

"Ah!" the pastor replied. "That's *really* a problem."

"What do you mean?" Walter said.

"Why, every person should be asking God and others, 'What can I do for you?'"

How would you have responded to Walter?

Do you ever feel that the whole world is seeking to TAKE from you?

When was the last time you asked honestly, "What more might I give?"

S
Supplementary Scriptures to Consider

The natural law of seedtime and harvest has been in place since the days of Noah:

The Lord said in the aftermath of the Great Flood:
"While the earth remains,
Seedtime and harvest,
Cold and heat,
Winter and summer,
And day and night
Shall not cease" (Genesis 8:22).

- Why do some people seem to expect "something from nothing" when the laws related to seedtime and harvest are universal and constant?

- Seedtime and harvest is a cycle that pertains to every aspect of life. Identify at least ten different and specific kinds of "seeds" that a person might plant—cover the spectrum of physical, material, financial, emotional, relational, mental, and spiritual "fields" in which a person might plant. What kinds of harvest might these seeds yield?

Good intentions about giving are not enough. Paul wrote to the Corinthians:

> As you abound in everything—in faith, in speech, in knowledge, in all diligence, and in your love for us—see that you abound in this grace also. . . . And in this I give advice: It is to your advantage not only to be doing what you began and were desiring to do a year ago; but now you also must complete the doing of it; that as there was a readiness to desire it, so there also may be a completion out of what you have. For if there is first a willing mind, it is accepted according to what one has, and not according to what he does not have (2 Corinthians 8:6, 10–12).

- What do you say to a person who argues that he or she does not have enough money at present to "give" any of it?

- How does Paul link "abounding" with giving?

Jesus taught:

> Give, and it will be given to you: good measure, pressed down, shaken together, and running over will be put into your bosom. For with the same measure that you use, it will be measured back to you" (Luke 6:38).

- Can a person ever out-give God?

- Is there ever a time when giving does not yield a harvest? What about a harvest in eternity?

- If a person desires a generous return, what is required?

I
Introspection and Implications

1. What is your attitude about giving? State in 25 words or less your prevailing opinion about giving.

2. Why is it important to remember at all times that it is God who "supplies seed to the sower"?

3. What is the result of giving generously? What does God desire from those who receive in abundance?

4. How much is "enough" to give? How much is "too much"?

C
Communicating the Good News

All ministry "costs" something—it may be time, the gift of talent, willing participation, money, material resources. How might a failure to evangelize be linked to a failure of giving?

What are you willing to give sacrificially for the winning of souls?

LESSON #7

GOD'S GRACE IS SUFFICIENT

Grace: God's infinite love, mercy, favor, and goodwill shown to mankind apart from mankind's deserving it Perils: exposure to great danger

B
Bible Focus

> *And lest I should be exalted above measure, by the abundance of the revelations, a thorn in the flesh was given to me, a messenger of Satan to buffet me, lest I be exalted above measure. Concerning this thing I pleaded with the Lord three times that it might depart from me. And He said to me, "My grace is sufficient for you, for My strength is made perfect in weakness." Therefore most gladly I will rather boast in my infirmities, that the power of Christ may rest upon me. Therefore I take pleasure in infirmities, in reproaches, in needs, in persecutions, in distresses, for Christ's sake. For when I am weak, then I am strong (2 Corinthians 12:7–10).*

We do not know the exact nature of Paul's thorn in the flesh. Some have conjectured that it was recurrent bouts of malaria, which can cause high fever and splitting headaches to the point of rendering a person temporarily blind. Others have theorized that it might have been seizures of some type, a strong temptation, or satanic persecution. What we can know with certainty is that his affliction was accompanied by intense and penetrating pain, and any person who has lived with prolonged or intense pain knows how debilitating and discouraging pain can be. This is true not only of physical pain, but also intense emotional, mental, or spiritual pain.

The question arises, of course: Why would God allow such an effective and powerful apostle to experience recurring suffering and pain?

Paul answers the question. He calls his thorn in the flesh a "messenger of Satan," specifically directed at Paul because he experienced an abundance of revelations from God. The exact nature of the "thorn" was unimportant to Paul, but the source and purpose of his affliction were very important. Satan was credited as being the source of his affliction. The purpose was that Paul might become either disillusioned about God or discouraged from sharing the deep spiritual insights that God had imparted to him. Paul clearly saw that there is danger any time a person feels blessed in a special way by God—such a person is likely to conclude that he is above the commandments of God or has been endowed with special privileges not available to other people. We must never draw either of those conclusions!

Paul also saw these times of affliction as being very important to his own understanding of God's grace and power. Paul discovered that God's grace completely covered or "eclipsed" his pain. Grace is God's love, favor, and blessings poured upon us apart from anything that we have done to earn them. Paul learned in his affliction that the glory of God's presence was more profound than Satan's influence, and the power of God was greater than the power of Satan. He came to understand that the victor in any situation is God and God alone. Name any problem you can and God is GREATER.

In the end, Paul knew that he emerged spiritually stronger and was a more potent witness for the Gospel as the result of His trusting God in times of affliction. We must not err in our interpretation of Paul's statement that he took "pleasure in infirmities, in reproaches, in needs, in persecutions, in distresses." Paul did not delight in pain and suffering. He did not seek out affliction. Rather, Paul liked the *outcome* of emerging victorious in Christ over affliction—Christ was honored and exalted, Christ's power was proven, and in these results, Paul rejoiced.

What important truths these are for us today!

When painful and debilitating afflictions strike us, we must be aware that God did not send the affliction. He may allow the affliction and He may use the affliction, but He is not the source of the affliction or temptation. God does not seek to harm His people, neither does He tempt them.

We must remain confident that God is with us in our affliction.

We must have faith to believe that God will give us the ability to endure our affliction.

We must be open to any and all lessons that God desires to teach us through our affliction.

And we must remain expectant that God will bring us out of our affliction.

Going through a tough time?

Turn to God and trust Him to bring you through it!

A
Application for Today

"This shouldn't have happened to me! I didn't do anything to deserve this," the young man complained to his older and wiser uncle, who had become his spiritual advisor over the years.

"Why do you think that you should have been spared this difficult experience?" his uncle asked.

"Because I have been doing everything I know to do to honor God and serve Him. If this is what a person gets for being a good Christian. . . ."

His uncle interrupted him.

"What a person gets for being a good Christian is an opportunity to be a good witness," his uncle said.

The young man sat back in his chair, a little stunned at his uncle's statement. "What do you mean?"

"Have you stopped to consider that God trusted you with this difficult experience so you might be an example to others that your faith is not just a good-times-and-blessings faith, but an always-and-forever faith?"

The young man thought for a moment and asked, "God *trusted* me with this?"

"Perhaps," his uncle replied. "People are watching you to see how you will respond, even if you are not aware of their watchful eyes. What you do in this time of trouble—how you trust God, how you respond to the situation, what you say and what you do—sends a strong message about your faith."

The young man was silent for a few moments. "But it hurts," he said with tears welling up in his eyes.

"Yes," his uncle said as he clasped his nephew's shoulder. "And that's why he put me in your life—to give you the privilege to cry."

Is there a difficult situation that God is entrusting to you as an opportunity to witness about His trustworthiness?

Is there someone who needs your comfort as he or she goes through a time of affliction? How might you best supply that comfort or encouragement?

S
Supplementary Scriptures to Consider

Paul's experiences with persecution and affliction were intense:

> Are they ministers in Christ?—I speak as a fool—I am more: in labors more abundant, in stripes above measure, in prisons more frequently, in deaths often. From the Jews five times I received forty stripes minus one. Three times I was beaten with rods; once I was stoned; three times I was shipwrecked; a night and a day I have been in the deep; in journeys often, in perils of waters, in perils of robbers, in perils of my own countrymen, in perils of the Gentiles, in perils in the city, in perils in the wilderness, in perils in the sea, in perils among false brethren; in weariness and toil, in sleeplessness often, in hunger and thirst, in fastings often, in cold and nakedness— besides the other things, which comes upon me daily: my deep concern fro all the churches. Who is weak, and I am not weak? Who is made to stumble, and I do not burn with indignation?
>
> If I must boast, I will boast in the things which concern my infirmity. The God and Father of our Lord Jesus Christ, who is

blessed forever, knows that I am not lying. In Damascus the governor, under Aretas the king, was guarding the city of the Damascenes with garrison, desiring to arrest me; but I was let down in a basket through a window in the wall, and escaped from his hands (2 Corinthians 11:22–33).

• From the very beginning, Paul seemed to attract persecution and suffering for the sake of the Gospel. Have you ever suffered on account of your witness for Christ Jesus? How so? What were the results in your life? What were the results in the lives of others around you? What were the results in the lives of those to whom you ministered?

• Many people seem to believe that because they are Christians, God should provide for them an easy life. Why is this never the case? Why is it that the stronger and more powerful a person's witness for Christ Jesus, the more troubles that person may experience?

• Do we ever do a disservice to new believers by not alerting them to the very real probability of their one day suffering because they have committed their lives to Christ Jesus?

Paul wrote this about suffering to the Colossians:

> I now rejoice in my sufferings for you, and fill up in my flesh what is lacking in the afflictions of Christ, for the sake of His body, which is the church, of which I became a minister according to the stewardship from God which was given to me for you, to fulfill the word of God, the mystery which has been hidden from ages and from generations, but now has been revealed to His saints (Colossians 2:24–26).

• Paul had a unique insight into the reason for his suffering as an apostle. He perceived that Jesus had suffered and died to "save" his Church, but that after the death of Jesus, the Church still needed to be built up, extended, and kept pure and faithful. This "ongoing" work of Christ involved suffering and sacrifice, just as the "saving" work of Christ involved suffering and sacrifice. To suffer in the service of Christ was not a penalty, but a privilege, for it was sharing in the ongoing life and ministry of Christ. Therefore, Paul "rejoiced" in his sufferings.

• Do you find it difficult to think of rejoicing and suffering being linked?

• Does the extension of the church, the edification or building up of the church, and efforts to keep the church faithful and pure always require an element of suffering and sacrifice? How do?

I
Introspection and Implications

1. Would you have been willing to suffer for Christ as Paul did? If not, to what degree do you believe you would be willing to suffer for Christ before you "threw in the towel"? What do you believe the Lord requires?

2. How are affliction and persecution different? (Note that affliction has a dimension of physical or mental distress.) In what ways are affliction and persecution similar?

3. What is the difference between seeking out suffering and being willing to suffer?

4. Paul used the phrase "a messenger from Satan to buffet me" in describing his afflictions. What does this phrase mean to you?

5. Is there a specific way in which God's strength has been "made perfect" in your weakness?

C
Communicating the Good News

The person who endures suffering for the Gospel with unwavering faith presents a powerful witness that God can be trusted in "bad times" as much as in "good times." In what specific ways do you believe suffering and persecution strengthen a person's witness?

Notes to Leaders
of Small Groups

As the leader of a small discussion group, think of yourself as a facilitator with three main roles:

- Get the discussion started

- Involve every person in the group

- Encourage an open, candid discussion that remains Bible focused

Remember, there may be a great diversity of knowledge among group participants. You certainly don't need to be the person with all the answers! In truth, much of your role is to be a person who asks questions:

- What really impacted you most in this lesson?

- Was there a particular part of the lesson, or a question, that you found troubling?

- Was there a particular part of the lesson that you found encouraging or insightful?

- Was there a particular part of the lesson that you'd like to explore further?

Express to the group at the outset of your study that your goal as group is to gain new insights into God's Word—this is not the forum for defending a point of doctrine or a theological opinion. Stay focused on what God's Word says and means. The purpose of the study is also to share insights on how to apply God's Word to everyday life. *Every* person in the group can and should contribute—the collective wisdom that flows from Bible-focused discussion is often very rich and deep.

Seek to create an environment in which every member of the group feels free to ask questions of other members in order to gain greater understanding. Encourage the group members to voice their appreciation to one another for new insights gained, and to be supportive of one another personally. Take the lead in doing this. Genuinely appreciate and value the contributions made by each person.

You may want to begin each study by having one or more members of the group read through the section provided under "Bible Focus." Ask the group specifically if it desires to discuss any of the questions under the "Application" section . . . the "Supplemental Scriptures" section . . . and the "Implications" and "Communicating the Gospel" section. You do not need to bring closure—or come to a definitive conclusion or consensus—about any one question asked in this study. Rather, encourage your group that if the group does not *have* a satisfactory Bible-based answer to a question that the group engage in further "asking . . . seeking . . . and knocking" strategies to discover the answers! Remember the words of Jesus: "Ask, and it will be given to you, seek, and you will find; knock, and it will be opened to you. For everyone who asks receives, and he who seeks finds, and to him who knocks it will be opened" (Matthew 7:7–8).

Finally, open and close your study with prayer. Ask the Holy Spirit, whom Jesus called the Spirit of Truth, to guide your discussion and to reveal what is of eternal benefit to you individually and as a group. As you close your study, ask the Holy Spirit to seal to your remembrance what you have read and studied, and to show you ways in the upcoming days, weeks, and months *how* to apply what you have studied to your daily life and relationships.

General Themes for the Lessons

Each lesson in this study has one or more core themes. Continually pull the group back to these themes. You can do this by asking simple questions, such as, "How does that relate to _____?", "How does that help us better understand the concept of _____?", or "In what ways does that help us apply the principle of _____?"

A summary of general themes or concepts in each lesson is provided below:

Lesson #1
ALL THINGS ARE "YES" IN CHRIST JESUS
Consistency
Trustworthiness
Absolute truth

Lesson #2

FORGIVENESS AND RESTORATION

Dealing with unfair, unwarranted criticism

Dealing with rumors and innuendo

Godly repentance

Forgiveness and mercy

Judgment and condemnation

Lesson #3

VICTORIOUS IN PERSECUTION

Dealing with persecution and suffering

Gaining right perspective in times of trial

How to deal with nagging "why God" questions

Dealing with persecutors or abusers

Lesson #4

ASSURANCE OF THE RESURRECTION

Mortality and immortality

Heavenly home

Death as a transition

Dealing with fear of death

Lesson #5

MARKS OF GENUINE MINISTRY

Christian ministry vs. social work

Marks of a mature believer in ministry

Lesson #6

GENEROSITY IN GIVING

Sacrificial giving vs. generous giving

The link between giving and receiving

The role of thanksgiving in giving

Lesson #7

GOD'S GRACE IS SUFFICIENT

God's purposes in allowing affliction, persecution, or suffering

The presence of God in times of affliction

The role of the enemy of our souls in affliction

God's trustworthiness at all times, in all situations

NOTES

NOTES

NOTES

NOTES

NOTES

NOTES

NOTES

NOTES

NOTES

NOTES

NOTES